YahYa's WORLD

AUTHOR - JOHN G. SMITH JR
ILLUSTRATOR - ALBON REID

Print information available on the last page

Rev. date: 08/23/2019

To order additional copies of this book, contact:
Xlibris
1-888-795-4274
www.Xlibris.com
Orders@Xlibris.com

BOOK DEDICATED TO ;   MY   GRAND   MAMAS

EARTH

Dust is on the earth
The air blows the dust
The wind blows the dust in the sky
The clouds are in the sky
Water is in the clouds
The clouds shall make the earth
The earth shall make the day.

BROTHER

I LOVE MY BROTHER ONLY,

IF I HAD ONE

MY BROTHER IS FUN TO PLAY

WITH

MY BROTHER HAS FUN GAMES

TO PLAY

MY BROTHER MAKES ME SMILE

MY BROTHER LOVES ME TOO,

ONLY IF I HAD A BROTHER !

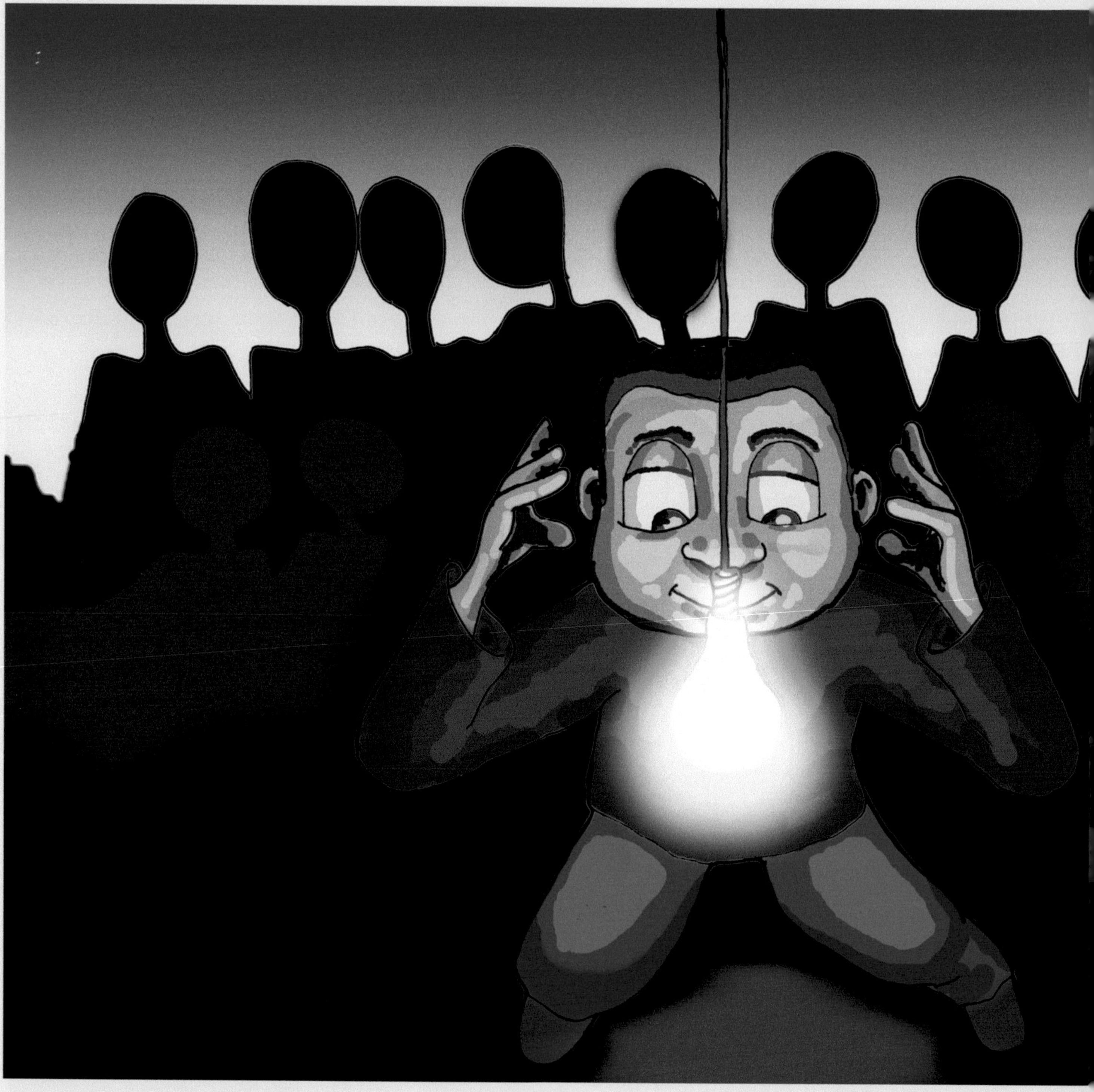

LIGHT

Light is pure
Light is bright
Light is light
Light is fun
I can see ...
I love light.

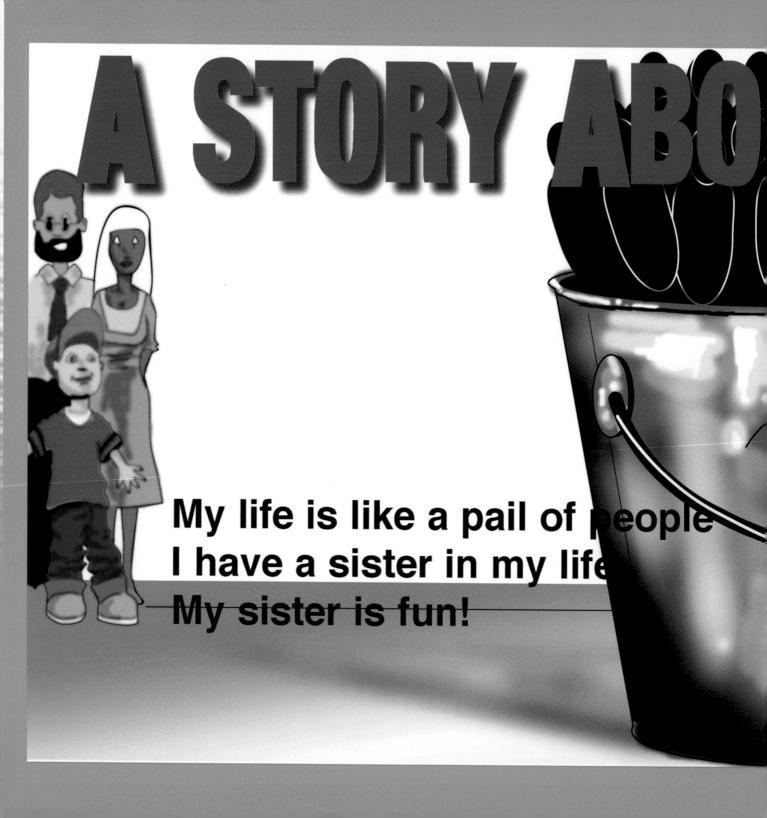

A STORY ABO

My life is like a pail of people
I have a sister in my life
My sister is fun!

T MY LIFE

She plays with me
when I don't have
anybody to play with
I have a mom and dad.
They are mean sometimes
and sometimes they nice

RT POEM

LUV U

My heart is your heart
My heart has love forever
My heart pleases me today
My heart loves the world
There is something I missed!
My heart also says, I love you!

THE HALLOWEEN BOY

Once there was a boy who loved Halloween!
Then one night his mother told him not to celebrate
Halloween
He said, to her, "Back Off"

The next night Halloween came
He celebrated, that night when he
went to bed, the Devil came and
took him!
Nobody ever saw him again!

Texas Tornado

In Texas a huge tornado hit. It blew everything. Then the chief said, "We are doomed"! So he ran before the tornado came back. But the Tornado found the chief. He got caught up in the tornado.

Now the people needed a new
chief. They found one.
He was a good chief. The next
day the tornado
came back! The new chief
stayed and faught the
tornado.

He helped people and won the
fight. Texas was saved!

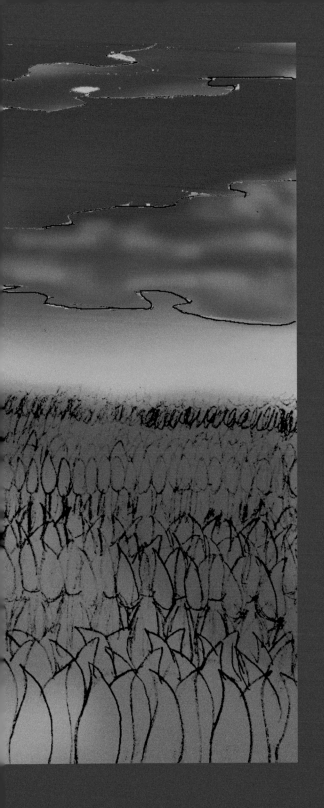

The sun is bright
The sun is warm

The sun is in the sky.
The sun is good

The sun makes vegetables
and plants grow

The sun is weather
The sun is above the
moon and stars.

Christmas Boy

Once there was a boy who loved christmas!
Every christmas he would help his family
clean and decorate everything!
On christmas eve he tried to stay up and see Santa.

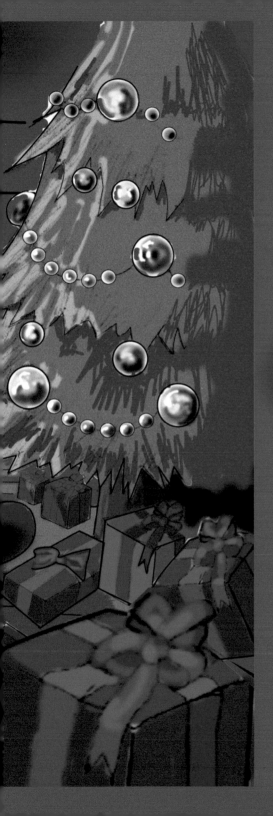

But, he always fell asleep. Then one christmas eve he stayed up and found Santa, he didn't get any presents because, he caught Santa!

Happy is happy
Happy is fun
Happy is good
Happy is pappy
Happy is wonder
Happy is strong
Happy is old
Happy is winter
Happy is freedom
Happy is free

Printed in the United States
By Bookmasters